From Egg to Adult
The Life Cycle of Birds

Heinemann
LIBRARY

Mike Unwin

www.heinemann.co.uk/library
Visit our website to find out more information about **Heinemann Library** books.

To order:
☎ Phone 44 (0) 1865 888066
📄 Send a fax to 44 (0) 1865 314091
🖥 Visit the Heinemann Bookshop at www.heinemann.co.uk/library to browse our catalogue and order online.

First published in Great Britain by Heinemann Library, Halley Court, Jordan Hill, Oxford OX2 8EJ, a division of Harcourt Education Ltd. Heinemann is a registered trademark of Harcourt Education Ltd.

Editorial: Nicole Irving and Georga Godwin
Design: Jo Hinton-Malivoire and AMR
Illustrations: David Woodroffe
Picture Research: Maria Joannou and Lizz Eddison
Production: Séverine Ribierre

Originated by Dot Gradations Ltd
Printed in China by Wing King Tong

ISBN 0 431 16863 6
07 06 05 04 03
10 9 8 7 6 5 4 3 2 1

British Library Cataloguing in Publication Data
Unwin, Mike
From egg to adult: The life cycle of birds
571.8'1157
A full catalogue record for this book is available from the British Library.

Acknowledgements
The Publishers would like to thank the following for permission to reproduce photographs:
Bruce Coleman Collection/Dr Eckart Pott p. **4**; Corbis pp. **5**, **10**, **13**; FLPA p. **22**; FLPA/David Hosking p. **18**; FLPA/Don Smith p. **15**; FLPA/J. Hawkins p. **14** (top); FLPA/M. Van Nostrand p. **12**; FLPA/Minden Pictures pp. **9**, **11**; FLPA/Peggy Heard p. **19**; FLPA/Roger Wilmshurst p. **25**; NHPA/A. P. Barnes p. **6**; NHPA/Bruce Beehler p. **21**; NHPA/Daniel Heuclin p. **26** (bottom); NHPA/Hellio & Van Ingen p. **7**; NHPA/Joe Blossom p. **16** (bottom); NHPA/Nigel J. Dennis p. **14** (bottom); NHPA/Stephen Dalton p. **26** (top); Oxford Scientific Films p. **16** (top); Oxford Scientific Films/Adrian Bailey p. **23**; Oxford Scientific Films/Ben Osbourne p. **17**; Oxford Scientific Films/Doug Alan p. **8**; Oxford Scientific Films/Gary & Terry Andrewartha p. **20**; Oxford Scientific Films/Michael Leach p. **24**.

Cover photograph of the black browed albatross family reproduced with permission of Steve Bloom.

The bird at the top of each page is a sandwill crane.

The author would like to thank Marianne Taylor for her invaluable assistance in the research and writing of this book.

The Publishers would like to thank Simon Butler for his assistance in the preparation of this book.

Every effort has been made to contact copyright holders of any material reproduced in this book. Any omissions will be rectified in subsequent printings if notice is given to the Publishers.

Contents

Look but don't touch: if you find a baby bird that seems to be lost, it is best to leave it alone. It is probably waiting for its parents to come and feed it. Look at it but do not touch it!

Any words appearing in bold, **like this**, are explained in the Glossary.

What is a bird?

Birds are animals that have two legs and two wings, and nearly all birds can fly. To help them fly, they have light, hollow bones and their skin is covered with feathers. Long feathers in their wings and tail are called flight feathers; these are necessary for flying. Smaller feathers, called **contour feathers**, cover their bodies. Tiny fluffy feathers underneath, called **down**, help them to keep warm. Birds are **vertebrates**, with bodies supported by a bone **endoskeleton**.

Central heating

Birds are **endothermic**, or 'warm-blooded', like mammals. This means that their bodies turn the food they eat into energy that keeps them warm, even when the air around them is cold. This is why birds can live in even the coldest parts of the world.

Pecking order

Birds don't have lips or teeth. They feed by using their beaks – sometimes called **bills**. The shape of a bird's beak is suited to the food that it eats. Finches have thick, strong beaks for cracking seeds, for example, while herons have long, pointed beaks for catching fish.

A swan has over 25,000 feathers on its body, more than any other bird.

How is a bird born?

All birds **reproduce** by laying eggs. Some, like the emperor penguin, lay just one egg. Others, like the grey partridge, may lay fifteen or more. Most birds lay one egg a day until the **clutch** of eggs is complete. Some, like the snowy owl, wait a few days after one egg before laying the next.

How big?

Eggs cannot be too big and heavy, or birds would not be able to fly with the eggs inside their body. Small birds usually lay smaller eggs. A bee hummingbird's egg weighs only 0.3 g – about the weight of a paper clip. The ostrich, which cannot fly, lays the biggest eggs of any bird. Each one is about the size of a coconut and weighs up to 1.9 kg – over 30 times the weight of a hen's egg (the kind we eat). An adult person can stand on an ostrich egg without breaking it.

Ostrich eggs have very thick shells. This means that they will not break when an adult ostrich sits down to **incubate** *them.*

Guillemots are seabirds that nest on narrow cliff ledges. Their eggs are cone-shaped, with rounded ends. This shape means that if the eggs are pushed, they spin round on the spot, and are less likely to roll off the cliff.

Shades and shapes

The colour and shape of eggs varies. Some birds, like the song thrush, lay blue eggs; others, like the peregrine falcon, lay reddish ones. Many birds that nest in holes, like kingfishers, lay white eggs, possibly so that the adult can see them more easily in the darkness. Most eggs are shaped like the chickens' eggs we eat, but some are more rounded, and some are more pointed.

How does an egg hatch?

Most birds lay their eggs on land. The hard shell prevents the soft insides from drying out. In the egg, the baby bird, or **embryo**, gets its food from the yolk. A cushion of thick liquid, called **amniotic fluid**, protects the yolk and embryo. The chickens' eggs that we eat contain yolk and amniotic fluid (the 'egg-white'), but no embryo, because they have not been **fertilized**.

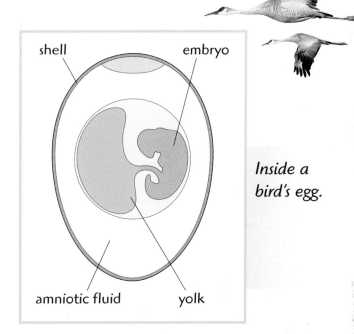

shell

embryo

amniotic fluid

yolk

Inside a bird's egg.

Keeping warm

Eggs must be kept warm for the embryo inside to grow. This is called **incubation**. Nearly all birds incubate their eggs by sitting on them. During this period, many also develop a bare patch of skin on their belly, called a **brood-patch**, through which they pass their body heat to the eggs. In some birds, the parents take it in turns to incubate the eggs. In others, one parent does it all. This is usually the female, but in a few birds it is the male.

Phalaropes breed in northern parts of the world, close to the Arctic Circle. Here, a male red-necked phalarope incubates the eggs while the female searches for food. Most birds do things the other way round.

Unusual incubations

Hornbills are fruit-eating birds, found in Africa and Asia, that nest in tree holes. Once the female has laid her eggs, she plasters over the entrance with mud to seal herself inside. She leaves just a small gap through which the male feeds her until the eggs hatch. Megapodes are ground-nesting birds found throughout Australia, New Zealand and the South Pacific. They cover their eggs with a mound of rotting vegetation. The male keeps the eggs at the right temperature for incubation by making the mound bigger or smaller.

Waiting for babies

The time it takes for eggs to **hatch** varies. This chart shows incubation times for a few different birds.

Bird	Incubation
royal albatross	80 days
king penguin	55 days
golden eagle	44 days
eider duck	24 days
zebra finch	12 days

Emperor penguins nest on the ice of Antarctica. The male carries the single egg on top of his feet, keeping it warm under a fold of skin on his belly like these penguins.

Protecting the eggs

Lots of **predators** like to eat birds' eggs, so the parents must protect them carefully. Some birds, such as plovers, lay **camouflaged** eggs, which look just like stones or sand. Many female birds, such as pheasants, are camouflaged themselves to protect them from predators while sitting on the eggs.

Defence and distraction

If predators approach the nest, the parents may try to chase them away. Arctic terns fiercely **dive-bomb** any animal that gets too close. The killdeer distracts predators like foxes by pretending to be injured. It calls loudly while running away from the nest and dragging one of its wings. The fox may decide to chase the killdeer instead of searching for the nest. The killdeer returns to its nest once the fox has gone.

This killdeer is just pretending to be injured in order to lure predators away from its nest.

What does a baby bird look like?

Some baby birds are weak, blind and featherless when they **hatch**. These are called **altricial** babies. Black-capped chickadee **nestlings** need to be kept warm by their parents for several days, until they have begun to grow feathers. They cannot feed themselves, so the parents bring their food back to the nest.

These black-capped chickadee nestlings do not grow their first feathers until they are five or six days old.

Let me out!

When a baby bird is ready to hatch, it taps on the inside of the eggshell with its beak. A special hard button on the end, called an **egg-tooth**, helps it to break through the shell. The egg-tooth disappears a few days after the chick has hatched.

Clearing up

When the chicks have hatched, the parents take the broken bits of eggshell away from the nest. Sometimes they even eat them. It is important that these broken shells do not remain in the nest; their white insides might attract the attention of predators looking for baby birds.

These mallard chicks have only been hatched for a few days, but they are covered in feathers and have already left the nest. They can see, swim and follow their mother to look for food.

Out and about

Other baby birds have a covering of **down** feathers and are able to see as soon as they hatch. These are called **precocial** babies. A newly hatched baby mallard can run, swim and feed by itself straight away. It still needs its mother to protect it from **predators** and to show it where food can be found.

Baby clothes

Even precocial baby birds do not look much like their parents at first. They have different markings and a different shape. It also takes at least two weeks before they grow their long wing and tail feathers like the adults. Adult avocets are black and white with long, upturned beaks, but their babies are plain grey with short, straight beaks.

Baby flamingos have small, straight beaks, like the one shown here. It takes them several months to develop the heavy, curved beak of an adult. They also have no flight feathers on their wings, so they cannot fly yet.

Looks aren't everything

Baby birds not only look different from their parents, they may also behave differently as well. Unlike their parents, mallard ducklings often dive under the water to look for food. The baby hoatzin is the only bird in the world with claws on its wings. It uses them to help it scramble around in the trees. The claws have disappeared by the time the hoatzin is an adult.

Who feeds baby birds?

These baby song thrushes are brought a constant supply of insects and other small animals by their parents.

Altricial baby birds are fed by their parents until they are big enough to leave the nest and find their own food. This means that the parents have a lot of work to do. A pair of black-capped chickadees may bring their chicks up to 1000 caterpillars a day!

Hungry mouths

Chicks beg their parents for food with high-pitched calls and wide-open mouths. This is called **gaping**. Some baby birds have brightly coloured markings inside their mouths called **gape spots**. This helps to guide the parents to their open mouths.

Pigeons regurgitate food directly into their chicks' mouths. The food is a liquid mixture of half digested seeds, called 'pigeon's milk'.

An easy meal

Some birds **regurgitate** food they have already swallowed for their chicks. This food is softer and easier for the chicks to manage. The herring gull feeds its chicks in this way. Adults have a red marking on their beak, which the chicks peck at when they want a parent to regurgitate some food.

Thirsty work

In hot, dry places, chicks need to drink regularly. Sandgrouse live in the desert, where water is scarce. Males visit waterholes and soak up water in special feathers on their bellies. They then fly back to the nest, up to 50 kilometres (30 miles) away. The chicks suck the water from the feathers.

Once they have drunk enough for themselves, sandgrouse soak their feathers in water to carry back to the nest.

A helping hand

It is not always just the parents who care for the chicks. In some birds, such as scrub jays, the parents share the work with one or more 'helpers'. These helpers are usually the parents' babies from the year before. They are not yet old enough to have babies of their own, so they help their parents instead.

Survival of the fattest

Baby birds are not always friendly to each other. Most eagles lay two eggs in a **clutch**, but usually only one chick survives to become an adult. This is because the bigger one bullies the smaller one and eats most of the food that the parents bring to the nest. It seems cruel, but this way, at least one chick is sure to grow up strong.

One strong, healthy eagle chick has a better chance of survival than two weaker ones.

When does a bird leave the nest and grow up?

Baby wood ducks fall a long way from the nest, but they land safely on the soft forest floor below.

Altricial birds stay inside the nest as they grow bigger and stronger. Eventually, when they get too big, their parents encourage them to leave. Many **precocial** birds, such as wood ducks, leave the nest straight away. Wood ducks nest in a tree hole. The ducklings cannot fly, so they have to jump to the ground. Their mother calls them down with a soft clucking sound.

Follow the leader

Precocial chicks become strongly attached to the first moving object they see when they **hatch** – usually their mother. This is called **imprinting**. It makes sure that the chicks stay close to their mother and follow her everywhere. If the chicks see another object or animal first, they become imprinted on that instead and ignore their real mother.

These baby chickens are imprinted on their mother. They will follow her wherever she goes.

A wandering albatross chick does not leave the nest or start to fly for almost a year after it hatches.

First flight

When a baby bird is ready to start flying, it is called a **fledgling**. Small birds like sparrows are able to fly about two weeks after hatching. Bigger birds take much longer. The wandering albatross is unable to fly until it is almost one year old.

How do parents protect their babies?

Even when newly hatched chicks can feed themselves, the parents still care for them in other ways. Baby swans and grebes ride on their parents' backs in the water. Baby avocets shelter from the cold under their parents' wings. Baby ostriches from several different parents all gather together to be looked after by just one or two adults, who protect them and chase **predators** away.

Learning the ropes

Fledglings learn the skills of flying, feeding, singing and keeping safe by watching adults. Peregrine parents encourage their chicks to fly by leaving the nest then calling them to follow. Chaffinches learn their songs from their parents. A chaffinch baby raised in **captivity**, that never hears its father singing, invents a different-sounding song of its own.

Reaching adulthood

It can take months or even years before a baby bird looks exactly like its parents. **Juvenile** European robins are brown all over. They do not have a red breast until they are grown-up. This helps to **camouflage** them while they are still learning to look after themselves. It also helps protect them from their fathers, since red is the **trigger** that makes adult male robins fight each other.

*When a young European robin develops its red breast, its father may attack it. To avoid trouble, the young robin leaves its parents' **territory** before the red breast feathers start to grow.*

Growing up fast

Some baby birds have to learn survival skills very quickly. Baby barn swallows born in June begin their long **migration** south in September. They will probably never see their parents again, but the following spring they will return to the exact same place where they were reared.

Slow start

Other birds take several years to reach adulthood. These include gulls and eagles. Each time a young eagle **moults**, its new set of feathers looks a little more like the adult's pattern. After a few years, it has grown the same **plumage** as its parents.

As they prepare to migrate south, these young swallows know nothing about the dangers that lie ahead. Many will not survive the journey, but those that do will have a better chance next time around.

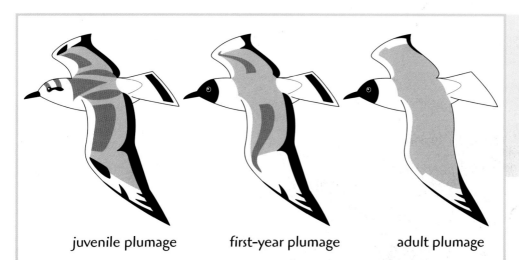

juvenile plumage   first-year plumage   adult plumage

Black-headed gulls take two years to reach full adult plumage.

19

When does a bird start breeding?

Birds start to **breed** in the spring. Usually, a male first finds an area with plenty of food and places to nest, and defends it from other males. This area is called a **territory**.

Why does a bird sing?

A male bird sings to attract females into his breeding territory and to keep other males away. Birdsong varies from the beautiful melody of the nightingale to the deep 'booming' call of the bittern. Birds that look very similar, such as the willow warbler and chiffchaff, have different-sounding songs so that the females don't get confused. The willow warbler's song is sweet and varied. The chiffchaff's is much more simple.

A male marsh warbler often imitates other birds during his long, complicated song.

Look at me!

Colourful birds, like peacocks, often **display** by jumping around or taking up strange positions to show off their breeding **plumage**.

20

The raggiana bird of paradise shows off his spectacular plumage in a dazzling song and dance display.

Do birds stay together forever?

Many birds find a new mate every year. Others, such as mourning doves, mate for life. A pair of gannets separates during the winter, because both birds head out to sea to find fish. However, they get back together at their breeding grounds each spring. When the two birds meet, they perform a **display** to show that they recognize each other and that the **bond** between them is still strong.

Who's best?

Male prairie chickens all display together. Females gather to watch, and choose the males with the best display to be their mates.

Male bowerbirds try to impress females by building large nest-like structures, and decorating them with bright objects.

Adelie penguins build their nests out of pebbles, so males offer females pebbles as a gift, to show that they are good at finding **nesting** material.

How does a bird build a nest?

Tailor-birds make a nest by stitching two big leaves together, using their beaks as needles and grass as thread.

The size and shape of nest varies from one bird to another. The white stork builds a huge nest of sticks, often on top of a chimney, which lasts for many years. Bee-eaters dig a tunnel in a riverbank to nest in, and woodpeckers make a hole in a tree trunk. Edible swiftlets make a tiny nest on the wall of a cave using their own sticky saliva (spit).

Safe at home

A bird's nest needs to be a safe place for the eggs and chicks. Most birds nest in a place that is hard for **predators** to reach. Some, such as the dunnock, nest deep in a thorny bush. Others, such as the bearded vulture, nest high on a cliff. The blue waxbill, a little African bird, nests close to bees' nests. The fierce stings of the bees help to keep predators away!

Building a home

Birds often share the job of nest building. In some species, however, one bird does all of the work. The male alone builds the complicated nests of weavers. Male wrens build the beginnings of several nests. The female picks one, and the pair finishes building this nest together.

Safety in numbers

Many birds live in groups or colonies. Having lots of nests close together helps them to protect each other from danger. Sociable weavers are small sparrow-like birds that live in the Kalahari Desert in southern Africa. They build one huge nest with many entrances all around, even at the bottom! This can provide a home for over three hundred birds.

Although sociable weavers only live for four or five years, one nest can last for over a hundred years. This may provide a home for many thousands of birds over that time.

The lazy solution

Some birds don't make their own nests. Burrowing owls take over the burrows of other animals such as ground squirrels to nest in. House sparrows sometimes use the nests of house martins, although they can build their own. A few birds do not use a nest at all. The fairy tern lays its single egg in a hollow in the branch of a tree.

The nest cheats

Some birds lay their eggs in other birds' nests. The female European cuckoo often lays her egg in the nest of a dunnock. She takes out one of the dunnock's own eggs so that there are the same number of eggs in the nest. The baby cuckoo **hatches** very quickly, and it pushes out the rest of the dunnock eggs. The adult dunnocks feed the baby cuckoo until it can fly.

Adult dunnocks don't seem to realize that the baby cuckoo they are feeding is not their own chick.

How long do birds live?

Birds do not have an easy life. They have to find enough food, avoid being caught by **predators** and some have to survive long **migration** journeys. Young birds are most at risk, and many will not survive to adulthood. In harsh winters, many birds die because they cannot find enough food. They need more food in cold weather because food gives them the energy they need to keep warm.

Food can be hard to find when snow is covering the ground. Fieldfares normally feed on insects, worms and snails, but in winter they rely on other food such as fallen apples.

What can you do to help?

There is plenty that people can do to make life easier for birds. Many birds survive cold winters thanks to people putting out birdseed for them in their gardens. Try this yourself – you might be surprised at how many different kinds of bird you can attract, even to a small garden. You can also put out nest boxes to help birds **breed** in spring.

A bird table should be placed out of the way of predators. A regular food supply will attract plenty of birds to your garden.

Oldest birds

Some of the oldest birds in the world live nearly as long as people. In **captivity**, some parrots and cockatoos can live for 60 years or even longer. The longest living birds are usually sea birds, because they have less predators. Albatrosses can live for over 50 years, while even small sea birds, such as storm petrels, can live to the age of 30.

The sulphur-crested cockatoo is a popular pet. It can live for over 80 years in captivity.

The cycle of life

No bird lives for ever. Even so, by the time an adult bird dies, it will have helped bring many more of its kind into the world. Over a lifetime, a female house sparrow may lay up to 120 eggs. Not all the eggs **hatch**, and many babies die young, but those that survive – if they overcome all the dangers of life, such as predators and cold winters – will grow up to have their own babies. This is the cycle of life – from egg to adult – in which young are born, grow up and produce young themselves. The cycle of life ensures the survival of each **species** of bird.

The life cycle of a bird

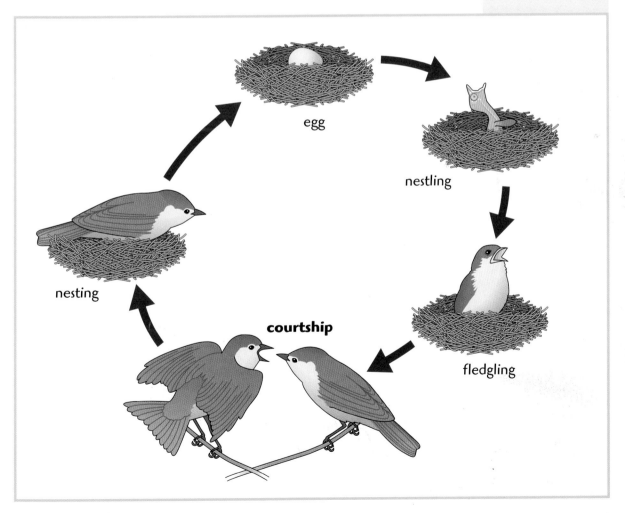

egg

nestling

courtship

nesting

fledgling

Fact file

What is ...

• the most eggs laid?
A bobwhite quail has laid a record **clutch** of 28 eggs. Grey partridges have the largest average clutch size of 15–19 eggs.

• the fewest eggs laid?
Albatrosses lay only one egg every two years.

• the fastest growing bird?
Some **species** of quail are fully grown-up and ready to breed only five weeks after **hatching**.

• the longest living bird?
The oldest known wild bird was a royal albatross at 58 years. In **captivity**, a sulphur-crested cockatoo lived for over 80 years.

• the furthest flying bird?
Arctic terns **migrate** from the Arctic to the Antarctic and back again every year. Some Arctic terns live for over 25 years and travel over one million km (620,000 miles) in their lives.

• the rarest bird in the world?
The last-known wild Spix's macaw disappeared from its rainforest home recently. Today, the only remaining Spix's macaws live in captivity. They became so rare because their habitat in Brazil was being destroyed, and because people captured the birds to sell them as pets.

Do birds' eggs ever contain more than one baby?

There is only room for one healthy baby bird to develop in an egg. Sometimes, however, hen's eggs that have not been **fertilized** are found with two or more yolks. The record is nine.

Bird classification

Classification is the way scientists group living things together according to features they have in common. There are over 9000 **species** of bird in the world. These are divided into many groups, according to the shapes of their bodies and the ways in which they live. Some of these groups are:

- **Birds of prey:** these have hooked beaks and sharp claws for hunting and eating meat. They include eagles, hawks and falcons. Owls are another group of hunting birds.

- **Herons:** these are big birds, with long legs and long, strong beaks. They usually live near water and hunt fish and other small animals. Other similar birds include storks and ibises.

- **Waders:** these birds have long legs and long, slender beaks, for catching worms and other small animals in mud or shallow water. They include sandpipers, curlews and avocets.

- **Waterfowl:** these are birds with webbed feet and flattened beaks that swim and find food in water. They include ducks, geese and swans.

- **Seabirds:** these spend most of their lives swimming in or flying over the sea. They include penguins, albatrosses, gulls, gannets and puffins.

- **Game birds:** these are seed-eating ground birds with plump bodies that prefer to run rather than fly. They include pheasants, quails, grouse and turkeys.

- **Parrots:** these birds have strong feet for climbing in trees, and powerful beaks for cracking nuts and seeds. This group also includes cockatoos, macaws and parakeets.

- **Perching birds:** most small songbirds are in this group, which is also known as the passerines. They include finches, warblers, thrushes, starlings and swallows.

Glossary

altricial baby birds that are blind, naked and helpless when they hatch

amniotic fluid thick liquid inside an egg that protects the embryo

bill another word for beak

bond close relationship between a breeding pair of birds

breed having babies

brood-patch unfeathered area on the belly of a bird, which helps during incubation

camouflaged coloured or patterned in a way that helps an animal blend in with its background

captivity being kept in one place, such as a zoo or cage, unable to get out

clutch group of eggs that are laid and incubated together in the same nest

contour feathers small feathers that cover the head and body of a bird

courtship special behaviour that takes place before mating

display dance or show of feathers used in courtship

dive-bomb fly fast at other animals, to scare them away

down soft fluffy feathers close to the skin that help keep a bird warm

egg-tooth hard button on the tip of a baby bird's beak, which helps it to hatch

embryo unborn young

endoskeleton skeleton of bones inside an animal's body

endothermic getting heat from inside the body

fertilize/fertilization when an egg is fertilized, an embryo begins to grow inside

fledgling baby bird that has just left the nest and begun to fly

gape spots markings found inside some baby birds' mouths, which encourage the parents to feed them

gaping opening the beak wide – baby birds do this to show their parents they need food

hatch break out of an egg

imprinting when baby birds follow the first moving thing they see after they hatch

incubation/incubate keeping eggs warm enough for the embryos inside to develop

juvenile young bird which is not yet ready to breed

migrate/migration seasonal journey of animals from one place to another in order to find food or a good place for breeding

moult when old feathers fall out and new ones grow in their place

nesting things birds use to build a nest, such as sticks, moss and feathers

nestling baby bird that is still in its nest and dependent on its parents

plumage all the feathers on a bird

precocial baby birds that can stand, run and feed themselves as soon as they have hatched